EVERYDAY DESSERTS MADE *Gourmet:*

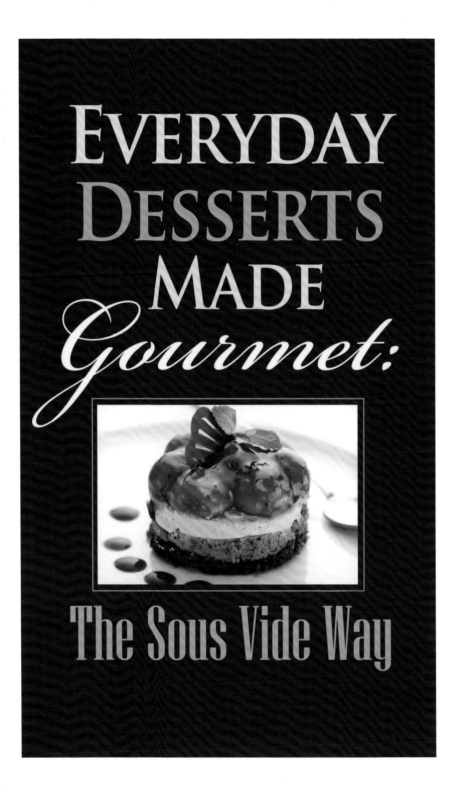

The Sous Vide Way

Printed in USA

© **Copyright 2013 KitchenAdvance**

ISBN 978-1-938653-10-0

Table of Content

Everyday Desserts made Gourmet: The Sous Vide way

Introduction

Gourmet Desserts are appealing, delicious and easy to prepare when using the Sous Vide method of cooking! Everyday Desserts Made Gourmet: The Sous Vide Way shows you how to transform desserts into culinary masterpieces – all cooked to perfection every time. Surprise your friends and family with a wide variety of scrumptious desserts that are sure to be a hit!

What is Sous Vide?

Sous Vide is a cooking method that has been long used in professional kitchens all around the world. In French *sous vide* means under vacuum. The method of cooking *sous vide* consists of three steps. First, food is sealed in airtight food bags. Then these bags are completely immersed in a water bath at a precisely-controlled temperature. The food cooks at its perfect finished temperature all the way through. The result is every item is cooked evenly from the inside-out and the outside-in.

Everyday Desserts
made
Gourmet:
The Sous Vide way

Why the AquaChef?

The **AquaChef Sous Vide Smart Cooker** is gourmet cooking made easy. No more worrying about overcooking your food or losing nutrients during the cooking process. The AquaChef enhances flavors and textures while cooking as the food remains sealed in with its own juices. Nothing is added and nothing is removed: there are no fats or oils added during the cooking process. Your food cooks in its own juices, at a precise temperature, creating perfect, delicious, and evenly cooked food from edge to edge.

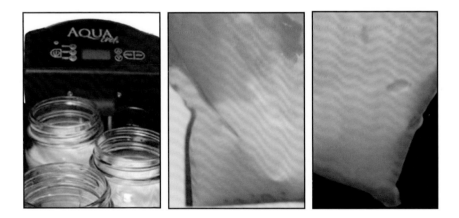

Dulce de leche

In Spanish, *Dulce de leche* means candy of milk or milk jelly. Originally popular in South America, Dulce de leche has recently increased in popularity in the United States as people discover its rich and sweet flavor. Dulce de leche is made by slowly heating sweetened milk to create a product that derives its taste from caramelized sugar. Slowly cooked Dulce de leche produces a milky jam product that is rich, satisfying and delicious. It's the perfect dessert for any occasion!

AquaChef Dulce de leche Apples

Time: 2 hours
Temperature: 175°F
Serves: 2

Items Needed:
vegetable peeler
mixing bowl
2 mason jars with lids

½ cup Dulce de leche sauce
   (recipe is on page 20)
2 large Granny Smith apples
2 tbs unsalted butter (melted)
½ tsp ground cinnamon

Prep:
Set up AquaChef by filling the water basin with 9 cups of water and turn on the AquaChef to preheat to 175°F. Begin by peeling the apples; once each is peeled cube each apple. Place cubed apples into the mixing bowl, add the melted butter, Dulce de leche sauce, and cinnamon. Combine all the ingredients and gently mix together. Once all combined divide the apples and place in each mason jar, cover each jar and place in the preheated AquaChef. Cook the AquaChef Dulce de leche Apples for 2 Hours at 175°F.

Finishing:
Carefully remove the AquaChef Dulce de leche Apples and serve with vanilla ice cream. Enjoy!

Dulce de leche Rice Pudding

Time: 2 hours
Temperature: 200°F
Serves: 4

1 cup short grain rice
1 ¾ cup half and half
¼ cup of water
¾ cup Dulce de leche sauce
½ tsp ground cinnamon
½ tsp vanilla extract
¼ cup of granulated sugar

Prep:
Set up AquaChef by filling the water basin to the max fill line with water and turn on the AquaChef to preheat to 200°F. Place the rice in a large Seal N Fresh bag, add the half and half, and the Dulce de leche sauce. Gently mix together. Add the remaining ingredients. Seal the top of the bag and gently agitate the bag. Place the sealed bag into the preheated AquaChef. Cook the Dulce de leche Rice Pudding for 2 hours at 200°F.

Finishing:
Carefully remove the Dulce de leche Rice Pudding and serve in heat safe bowl. Enjoy!

Dulce de leche Sauce

Time: 4 hours
Non-Cook Time: 2 hours
Temperature: 175°F
Serves: 4

1 can of sweetened condensed milk

Items Needed:
can opener

Prep:
Set up AquaChef by filling the water basin with water to the max fill line and turn on the AquaChef to preheat to 175°F.

Empty the sweetened condensed milk into a Seal N Fresh bag and seal the top of the bag, place the bag in the preheated AquaChef.

Finishing:
Once the Dulce de leche Sauce is done let cool slightly, serve with your favorite dessert. Enjoy!

Tips:
This easy caramel in a can will be used in the Caramel Apple Bread Pudding.

Panna cotta

Panna cotta is an Italian dessert cooked with cream, milk, sugar and gelatine. It's simple, yet delicious and can be topped and served with a variety of different fruits and sauces. Panna cotta is a light and flavorful summer dessert!

AquaChef Panna cotta

Time: 20 minutes
Non Cooking Time: 8-10 hours
Temperature: 165°F
Serves: 2-4

Items Needed:
measuring cups
measuring spoons
ramekins
metal sieve
measuring cup/bowl with lip
  for easy pouring
mixing spoon

1 cup heavy whipping cream
½ cup half & half
½ tsp vanilla extract
¼ cup granulated sugar
¼ cup half & half
  (for softening the gelatine)
1 packet unflavored gelatine

Prep:
Set up AquaChef by filling the water basin with water to the max fill line and turn on the AquaChef to preheat to 165°F.

In a small Seal N Fresh Bag place the heavy whipping cream, 1/2 cup half & half, vanilla, and sugar.

Seal the top of the bag and mix around with your hand. Place the bag in the preheated AquaChef.

Once the bag is heating inside the AquaChef pour the unflavored gelatine into the remaining 1/4 cup of half & half and lightly mix.

Continue on next page...

AquaChef Panna cotta (continued)

Set aside the gelatine and half & half mixture. Let stand together for 5-10 minutes. Once the cream in the AquaChef has thoroughly heated add the gelatine and half & half mixture, seal the top of the bag and gently mix around. Once mixed together pour into a measuring cup/ bowl with lip (for easy pouring) through a metal sieve.

Pour the AquaChef Panna cotta into your ramekins. Depending on the size of your ramekins you can fill 2-4. Place in the refrigerator for 8-10 hours to set.

Finishing:
Once set gently run a warm paring/butter knife around the rim of the panna cotta. Place the ramekin in warm water for 10-15 seconds. Then invert onto a plate and serve with the strawberry sauce (page 99). Enjoy!

Tips:
When removing the AquaChef Panna cotta from ramekins be sure you have it exactly where you want it on the plate as it does not move easily. You can also serve in decorative glasses if you do not want to worry about removing the AquaChef Panna cotta.

AquaChef Panna cotta

Coffee Panna cotta

Time: 20 Minutes
Non Cooking Time: 8-10 hours
Temperature: 165°F
Serves: 2-4

Items Needed:
measuring cups
measuring spoons
ramekins
fine metal sieve
measuring cup/ bowl with
   spout/lip for easy pouring
mixing spoon

1 cup heavy whipping cream
½ cup half & half
3 tbs coffee grounds
   (any that you choose)
½ tsp vanilla extract
¼ cup granulated sugar
¼ cup half & half
   (for softening the gelatine)
1 packet unflavored gelatine

Prep:
Set up AquaChef by filling the water basin with water to the max fill line and turn on the AquaChef to preheat to 165°F. In a small Seal N Fresh bag place the heavy whipping cream, half & half, coffee grounds, vanilla, and sugar. Seal the top of the bag and mix around with your hand; place the bag in the preheated AquaChef for 20 minutes.

While the bag is heating inside the AquaChef pour the unflavored gelatine into the remaining 1/4 cup of half & half and lightly mix. Set aside the gelatine and half & half mixture. Let stand together for 5-10 minutes.

Continue on next page...

Coffee Panna cotta (continued)

Once the cream in the AquaChef has thoroughly heated add the gelatine and half & half mixture, seal the top of the bag and gently mix around. Once mixed together pour into a measuring cup/bowl with spout/lip (for easy pouring) through a metal sieve. Pour the AquaChef Panna cotta into your ramekins; depending on the size of your ramekins you can fill 2-4. Place into the refrigerator for 8-10 hours to set.

Finishing:

Once set gently run a warm paring/butter knife around the rim of the panna cotta, place the ramekin in warm water for 10-15 seconds. Then invert onto a plate and serve with chocolate sauce. Enjoy!

Tips:

If you like the coffee flavor to be more or less intense adjust to your liking.

Coffee panna cotta

Raspberry Panna Cotta

Time: 30 minutes
Non Cooking Time: 8-10 hours
Temperature: 165°F
Serves: 2-4

Items Needed:
measuring cups
measuring spoons
ramekins; fine metal sieve
measuring cup/ bowl with lip
  for easy pouring
mixing spoon
small whisk

for Raspberry compote:
  1 6oz package fresh raspberries
  2 tbs granulated sugar
for Panna cotta:
  1 cup heavy cream
  ¼ cup half & half
  2 tbs sugar
  ¼ tsp vanilla extract
strained Raspberry compote
  (about ½ cup, if a little more that is fine)
1 package unflavored gelatine

Prep:
Set up AquaChef by filling the water basin with water to the max fill line and turn on the AquaChef to preheat to 165°F. Start by rinsing the fresh raspberries and letting them dry. Once dry place the raspberries in a small Seal N Fresh bag with 2 tbs of granulated sugar. Seal the bag with the Seal N Fresh vacuum sealer. Place the bag in the preheated AquaChef and cook for 15 minutes. Once the raspberries are done remove from bag and strain using the metal sieve into a small bowl. This compote will be used to bloom the gelatine into. Start the panna cotta by placing the heavy cream, half & half, sugar, and vanilla extract into a Seal N Fresh bag.

Continue on next page...

Raspberry Panna Cotta (continued)

Seal the top of the bag and place in the preheated AquaChef for 15 minutes. While the Panna cotta is heating begin to bloom the unflavored gelatine in the Raspberry compote. Once the Panna cotta is done heating open the bag and add the raspberry gelatine and gently whisk together. Once mixed, strain into container with spout/lip (for easy pouring). Pour the Raspberry Panna cotta into your ramekins; depending on the size of your ramekins you can fill 2-4. Place into the refrigerator for 8-10 hours to set.

Finishing:
Once set gently run a warm paring/butter knife around the rim of the Raspberry Panna cotta, place the ramekin in warm water for 10-15 seconds. Then invert onto a plate and serve with chocolate sauce or whipped cream. Enjoy!

Tips:
If you are not able to use fresh raspberries frozen can be used, 1 ¼ cup frozen.

Raspberry

Panna Cotta

Custard

&

Crème Anglaise

Custard is a mixture of sugar, egg yolks and hot milk. Depending on how much egg or thickener is used, custard may vary in consistency from a thin pouring sauce (*crème anglaise*), to the thick pastry cream used to fill éclairs. However, custard preparation is a delicate operation, because a temperature increase of 5–10 °F (3-6 °C) leads to overcooking and curdling. Thus, because of its precision temperature control, the *sous vide* method is the ideal way to cook custards!

AquaChef Vanilla Creme Anglaise

Time: 25 minutes
Non Cooking Time: 2-4 hours
Temperature: 175°F
Serves: 3-4

3 egg yolks
½ cup heavy cream
½ cup half & half
½ vanilla bean
¼ cup granulated sugar

Items needed:
small mixing bowl
whisk; metal sieve
rubber spatula
plastic wrap

Prep:
Set up AquaChef by filling the water basin with water to the max fill line and turn on the AquaChef to preheat to 175°F.

In small Seal N Fresh bag add the egg yolks and gently whisk. Add the heavy cream, half & half, vanilla bean, and sugar. Seal the top of the bag and mix around the ingredients and place in the pre-heated AquaChef. Cook the AquaChef Vanilla Creme Anglaise for 25 Minutes at 175°F.

Finishing:
Carefully remove the Vanilla Anglaise and using a metal sieve strain into a small mixing bowl. Once strained cover with plastic wrap and refrigerate for 2-4 hours. Serve with your favorite desserts. Enjoy!

Tips:
This delicious dessert sauce makes a great base for homemade ice cream.

AquaChef Vanilla Custard

Time: 1 hour
Temperature: 180°F
Serves: 3

Items Needed:
hand mixer or stand mixer
mixing bowls
strainer or food sieve
3-4 half pint mason jars or
8 oz ramekins

1 cup heavy whipping cream
½ vanilla bean
½ cup granulated sugar
2 whole large eggs
4 large egg yolks
pinch of salt

Prep:
Set up AquaChef by filling the water basin with 9 cups of water and turn on the AquaChef to preheat to 180°F. Place heavy whipping cream in mixing bowl, scrape the inside of the vanilla bean and place in the mixing bowl. Add the remaining ingredients into the mixing bowl and gently mix the ingredients together being sure all are incorporated but being careful not to mix until frothy. Strain mixture into clean mixing bowl or large measuring cup. Pour mixture into mason jars or ramekins being sure not to overfill each. Cover each and place in the preheated AquaChef. Cook the AquaChef Vanilla Custard for 1 hour at 180°F.

Finishing:
Remove the AquaChef Vanilla Custard and let cool in the refrigerator for 4-6 hours. Serve alone or with fresh fruit. Enjoy!

Tips:
If you do not use vanilla bean you can substitute 1 teaspoon vanilla extract.

Butterscotch Custard

Time: 1 hour
Non Cook Time: 4-6 hours
Temperature: 180°F
Serves: 4

Items Needed:
saucepan
hand mixer or stand mixer
mixing bowls
strainer or food sieve
4 half pint mason jars or 8 oz
  ramekins
4 mason jar lids

¾ cup heavy whipping cream
½ tsp vanilla extract
¼ cup granulated sugar
2 whole large eggs
4 large egg yolks
pinch of salt
butterscotch sauce:
  ¼ cup heavy whipping cream
  3/4 cup butterscotch morsels

Prep:
Set up AquaChef by filling the water basin with 9 cups of water and turn on the AquaChef to preheat to 180°F.

Place heavy whipping cream in mixing bowl. Add vanilla extract, sugar, egg yolks, eggs, and salt to the mixing bowl and gently mix the ingredients together being sure all are incorporated but being careful not to mix until frothy. Set aside. In saucepan heat cream for butterscotch sauce.

Place the butterscotch morsels in a heat safe bowl. Once the cream is starting to bubble remove from the heat and add to the butterscotch morsels . Mix together until smooth.

Continue on next page...

Butterscotch Custard (continued)

Temper the sauce into the plain custard by adding some of the plain custard to the butterscotch sauce. Then incorporate both together.

Strain mixture into clean mixing bowl or large measuring cup. Pour mixture into mason jars or ramekins being sure not to overfill. Cover each and place in the preheated AquaChef.

Cook the Butterscotch Custard for 1 Hour at 180°F.

Finishing:
Carefully remove the Butterscotch Custard from the AquaChef and refrigerate for 4-6 hours before serving. Serve with whipped cream. Enjoy!

Tips:
This dessert will be a great addition to any holiday dinner! Serving with ginger snap cookies makes this dessert extra festive.

Butterscotch Custard

Chocolate Custard

Time: 1 hour
Non Cooking Time: 4-6 hours
Temperature: 180°F
Serves: 4

Items Needed:
saucepan
hand mixer or stand mixer
mixing bowls
strainer or food sieve
4 half pint mason jars or
   8 oz ramekins
4 mason jar lids

¾ cup heavy whipping cream
½ vanilla bean
¼ cup granulated sugar
2 whole large eggs
4 large egg yolks
pinch of salt
chocolate ganache:
   ¼ cup heavy whipping cream
   ½ cup semisweet chocolate
   chips

Prep:

Set up AquaChef by filling the water basin with 9 cups of water and turn on the AquaChef to preheat to 180°F.

Place heavy whipping cream in mixing bowl. Scrape the inside of the vanilla bean and place in the mixing bowl. Add the next four ingredients and gently mix the ingredients together being sure all are incorporated but being careful not to mix until frothy. Set aside.

In saucepan heat cream for ganache. Place the semisweet chocolate chips in a heat safe bowl. Once the cream is starting to bubble remove from the heat and add to the chocolate chips. Mix together until smooth.

Continue on next page...

Chocolate Custard (continued)

Temper the chocolate ganache into the plain custard by adding some of the plain custard to the chocolate, then incorporate both together. Strain mixture into clean mixing bowl or large measuring cup.

Pour mixture into mason jars or ramekins being sure not to overfill. Cover each and place in the preheated AquaChef.

Cook the Chocolate Custard for 1 hour at 180°F.

Finishing:
Remove the Chocolate Custard and let cool in the refrigerator for 4-6 hours. Serve alone or with Strawberry Sauce. Enjoy!

Eggnog Creme Anglaise

Time: 25 minutes
Non Cooking Time: 2-4 hours
Temperature: 165°F
Serves: 3-4

Items needed:
small mixing bowl
whisk
metal sieve
rubber spatula
plastic wrap

3 egg yolks
½ cup heavy cream
3/4 cup half & half
½ tsp vanilla extract
2 tbs dark rum
3-5 whole cloves
¼ tsp ground nutmeg
¼ tsp ground cinnamon
¼ cup granulated sugar

Prep:
Set up AquaChef by filling the water basin with water to the max fill line and turn on the AquaChef to preheat to 165°F. Using the mixing bowl, add the yolks and cream and whisk together. Add the half and half. Add the remaining ingredients and gently whisk together. Place the combined ingredients into a Seal N Fresh bag, seal the top of the bag and place in the preheated AquaChef.

Cook the Eggnog Creme Anglaise for 25 minutes at 165°F.

Finishing:
Carefully remove the Eggnog Creme Anglaise. Using a metal sieve strain into a small mixing bowl. Once strained cover with plastic wrap and refrigerate for 2-4 hours. Serve with the Eggnog Bread Pudding. Enjoy!

Pumpkin Custard

Time: 1 hour
Temperature: 180°F
Serves: 2

Items Needed:
mixing bowl
rubber spatula
whisk
2 ramekins or mason jars

1 cup pumpkin puree
2 large eggs
1 large egg yolk
1 tsp pumpkin pie spice
½ tsp ground cinnamon
¼ cup granulated sugar
½ tsp vanilla extract
½ cup coconut milk

Prep:
Set up AquaChef by filling the water basin with water to the minimum fill line and turn on the AquaChef to preheat to 180°F.

In mixing bowl place pumpkin puree; add eggs and yolk. Mix the ingredients together. Add pumpkin pie spice, cinnamon, sugar, and vanilla extract. Mix until sugar is dissolved. Add coconut milk and mix for another minute or until all the ingredients are incorporated.

Divide the mixture and place in ramekins or mason jars. If using mason jars cover with lids.

Place each in the preheated AquaChef. Cook the Pumpkin Custard for 1 Hour at 180°F.

Continue on next page...

Pumpkin Custard (continued)

Finishing:

Carefully remove the custard and place in ice bath. Once cooled refrigerate for 3-4 hours. Optional serve with whipped topping. Enjoy!

Tips:

Be sure to use pumpkin puree not pumpkin pie mix in a can.

Yogurt

Yogurt is an age-old dairy product produced by bacterial fermentation of milk. The perfect temperature control provided by the *sous vide* method makes it the ideal way to produce this healthy dish. Nutritionally rich in protein, calcium, riboflavin, vitamin B6 and vitamin B12, yogurt is a tasty, healthy and versatile dish that can be used for anything from sauces to desserts.

AquaChef Yogurt

Time: 12 hours
Temperature: 185°F, 122°F, and 100°F
Serves: 2 per jar

Items Needed:
thermometer (digital preferred)
3-4 17 oz mason jars (We fit 4 jars snugly in our AquaChef)

16 oz of milk per mason jar (<u>DO NOT</u> use ultra pasteurized milk)
Any % that you prefer is fine (we used 1%)
2 tbs plain yogurt with active cultures per mason jar (leave out at room temp)
1 tsp plain white sugar per mason jar

Prep:
Set up AquaChef by filling the water basin with water to the max fill line and turn on the AquaChef to preheat to 185°F.

Clean both the tops and mason jars that will be used. Once the jars are clean and dry add milk being sure to leave room to stir and add yogurt starter. Place each jar in the AquaChef and top each with a lid but do not tighten the lid.

Cook for a minimum 1 hour, using the thermometer. Check the milk to make sure it has reached an internal temperature of 185°F.

Continue on next page...

AquaChef Yogurt (continued)

Once the Milk has reached this temperature remove some of the water being extremely careful and add ice cubes to cool the milk to 122°F. Once the temperature reaches 122°F stir 2 tbs of yogurt and 1 tsp of white sugar into each mason jar.

Loosely cover each jar and set the AquaChef to 100°F and set the time for 10 hours.

Finishing:
Remove each mason jar. Seal each jar and place in an ice bath to stop the cultures from growing. Place in the refrigerator and store for up to two weeks. Serve in smoothies or with honey. Enjoy!

Tips:
You can use your AquaChef yogurt as the yogurt starter the next time you make yogurt. Also you can have your yogurt incubate longer if you wish to have a more sour and tangy yogurt. (No more than 24 hours of incubation is suggested).

Cakes

There are countless cake recipes. Some are bread-like, some rich and elaborate, and many are centuries old. Here we show how to use the *sous vide* way to create rich flavors and textures, plus some easy and delicious cheesecakes as well!

Berry Cheesecake

Time: 2 hours
Temperature: 165°F
Serves: 2

Items Needed:
stand or hand mixer
small bowl
rubber spatula
2 ramekins or mason jars

8 oz package of cream cheese
@ room temperature
2 tbs granulated sugar
½ tsp vanilla extract
2 tbs all purpose flour
1 large egg
1 large egg yolk
1 cup frozen mixed berries
1 tsp all purpose flour for
coating the berries

Prep:
Set up AquaChef by filling the water basin with water to the minimum fill line and turn on the AquaChef to preheat to 165°F.

Using stand mixer or hand mixer place cream cheese in small bowl and mix for 1-2 minutes alone.

Add the granulated sugar, vanilla extract, and flour. Mix well being sure all ingredients are incorporated.

Scrape down the bowl and add the egg. Make sure it is completely incorporated before adding the yolk. Add the yolk and set aside.

In a separate bowl place frozen berries and remaining flour and toss, coating the berries in the flour.

Continue on next page...

Berry Cheesecake (continued)

Gently fold in the flour coated berries and divide between the ramekins/mason jars.

If using mason jars cover with mason jar lids. Place each in the preheated AquaChef. Cook the Berry Cheesecake for 2 hours at 165°F.

Finishing:
Carefully remove the Berry Cheesecakes and place in the refrigerator to cool for a few hours or overnight. Enjoy!

Corn Bread Pudding Cake

Time: 1 hour 30 minutes
Temperature: 185°F
Serves: 2-4

Items Needed:
mixing bowl
whisk
rubber spatula
grater
ramekin/mason jars

1 box of Jiff Cornbread mix
½ cup creamed corn
2 large egg yolks
2 tbs unsalted butter (melted)
2 tbs shredded cheddar cheese
toppings:
　sour cream
　chopped chives

Prep:
Set up AquaChef by filling the water basin with 9 cups of water and turn on the AquaChef to preheat to 185°F.

Begin by emptying the cornbread mix into the mixing bowl, breaking up any clumps with the whisk.

Add the creamed corn, egg yolks, and melted butter. Mix together using the rubber spatula.

Once all is incorporated add the shredded cheese and gently fold into the batter.

Continue on next page...

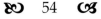

Corn Bread Pudding Cake (continued)

Divide the batter into each ramekin/mason jar. Be sure not to fill more than ¾ of the way full.

Cover each filled mason jar with mason jar lid.

Place each filled ramekin/mason jar into the preheated AquaChef.

Cook the Corn Bread Pudding Cake for 1 Hour and 30 Minutes at 185°F.

Finishing:

Carefully remove the Corn Bread Pudding Cake and serve with a dollop of sour cream and chopped chives. Enjoy!

Date and Walnut Cheesecake

Time: 1 hour
Non Cooking Time: 6-8 hours
Temperature: 165°F
Serves: 2

Items Neeed:
stand or hand
mixer
small bowl
rubber spatula
2 ramekins or mason jars

8 oz cream cheese
2 tbs granulated sugar
1 tsp ground cinnamon
½ tsp vanilla extract
2 tbs all purpose flour
1 large egg
1 large egg yolk
½ cup chopped dates
½ cup chopped walnuts
1 tsp all purpose flour (for
     coating the dates and walnuts)

Prep:
Set up AquaChef by filling the water basin with water to the minimum fill line and turn on the the AquaChef to preheat to 165°F.

Using stand mixer or hand mixer mix cream cheese for 1-2 minutes alone.

Add the granulated sugar, cinnamon, vanilla extract, and flour. Mix well being sure all ingredients are incorporated.

Scrape down the bowl and add the egg, making sure it is completely incorporated before adding the yolk. Add the yolk and make sure to mix well, set aside.

Continue on next page...

Date and Walnut Cheesecake (continued)

In small bowl place the chopped dates and walnuts. Add 1 Tsp of all purpose flour and toss the dates and walnuts with the flour.

Once the dates and walnuts are coated with the flour gently fold into the cheesecake batter.

Once all incorporated divide the batter into the two ramekins or mason jars. Place in the preheated AquaChef.

Cook the Date and Walnut Cheesecake for 1 hour at 165°F.

Finishing:
Carefully remove the Date and Walnut Cheesecake from the AquaChef. Before serving place in refrigerator for 6-8 hours. Enjoy!

Date and Walnut

Cheesecake

Fire Roasted Bell Pepper Ricotta Cheesecake

Time: 2 hours
Temperature: 165°F
Serves: 2

Items Needed:
stand or hand mixer
mixing bowl
rubber spatula
2 ramekins or ½ pint mason
  jars

2 oz fire roasted bell peppers
10 oz ricotta cheese
3 tbs all purpose flour
1 large egg
1 large egg yolk
½ tsp minced garlic
salt and pepper to taste

Prep:
Set up AquaChef by filling the water basin with 9 cups of water
and turn on the AquaChef to preheat to 165°F.

First julienne the fire roasted bell peppers and line the bottom
of each ramekin/mason jar. Set aside while you make the ricotta
cheese cake batter.

Using the stand or hand mixer place the ricotta cheese, flour, eggs,
garlic, and salt and pepper in the mixing bowl. Mix the ingredients
for 2 minutes, scrape down the bowl and mix for 1 more minute.

Divide the batter and fill the ramekins/ mason jars with the ricotta
batter being sure not to overfill.

Continue on next page...

Fire Roasted Bell Pepper Ricotta Cheesecake (continued)

Prep:
If you are using mason jars cover with mason jar lids. Place each in the preheated AquaChef.

Cook the Fire Roasted Bell Pepper Ricotta Cheesecake for 2 hours at 165°F.

Finishing:
Carefully remove and place in an ice bath, then chill for 3-6 hours in the refrigerator. Enjoy!

Tips:
This savory treat makes a great appetizer for a party. Serve with pita chips and enjoy!

Gingerbread Pudding Cake

Time: 1 hour 30 minutes
Temperature: 195°F
Serves: 2

Items Needed:
stand or hand mixer
mixing bowl
rubber spatula
2 ramekins

wet ingredients:
½ cup unsalted butter
@ room temperature
2 tbs granulated sugar
pinch of salt
¼ cup dark molasses
1 large egg

dry ingredients:
½ cup all purpose flour
½ tsp ground ginger
½ tsp ground cinnamon
¼ tsp chinese 5 spice
¼ cup chopped
candied ginger

Prep:
Set up AquaChef by filling the water basin with 9 cups of water
and turn on the AquaChef to preheat to 195°F.

Using a stand or hand mixer begin to cream the butter, sugar, and
salt together until light and fluffy.

Scrape down the bowl using the rubber spatula. Add the molasses
and mix well, make sure the molasses is well incorporated before
adding the egg.

Continue on next page...

Gingerbread Pudding Cake (continued)

Add the egg and make sure it is completely incorporated before adding the dry ingredients.

In separate bowl mix flour, ground ginger, cinnamon, and chinese 5 spice.

Slowly add the the dry ingredients to the wet ingredients. Once all is incorporated gently fold in the chopped candied ginger.

Divide the batter and place into the ramekins. Place in the preheated AquaChef.

Cook the Gingerbread Pudding Cake for 1 hour 30 minutes at 195°F.

Finishing:
Carefully remove the Gingerbread Pudding Cake. Serve with whipped cream. Enjoy!

Pineapple and Apricot Pudding Cake

Time: 1 hour 30 minutes
Temperature: 180°F
Serves: 2

Items Needed:
stand or hand mixer
mixing bowl
rubber spatula
2 ramekins

wet ingredients:
¼ cup unsalted butter,
@ room temperature
2 tbs granulated sugar
pinch of salt
¼ cup pineapple curd (recipe
on page 118)
1 large egg
¼ cup crushed pineapple
3 tbs chopped dried apricot
dry ingredients:
½ cup all purpose flour

Prep:
Set up AquaChef by filling the water basin with 9 cups of water
and turn on the AquaChef to preheat to 180°F.

Using stand or hand mixer cream the butter and sugar together
until light and fluffy.

Scrape down the sides of the bowl, add salt and pineapple curd.
Be sure all ingredients are incorporated before adding more.

Scrape down the bowl with the rubber spatula and add the egg.

After the egg is incorporated add the crushed pineapple and
chopped apricots, mix together until all is incorporated.

Continue on next page...

Pineapple and Apricot Pudding Cake
(continued)

Prep:
Divide the batter and place in the ramekins.

Place each ramekin into the preheated AquaChef. Cook the Pineapple and Apricot Pudding Cake for 1 hour and 30 minutes at 180°F.

Finishing:
Carefully remove the Pineapple and Apricot Pudding Cake. Optional: serve with pineapple curd and whipped cream. Enjoy!

Everyday Desserts
made
Gourmet:
The Sous Vide way

Pineapple Coconut Cheesecake

Time: 2 hours
Non-Cook Time: 6-8 hours
Temperature: 165°F
Serves: 2

Items Needed:
stand or hand mixer
small bowl
rubber spatula
2 ramekins or mason jars

8 oz package of cream cheese
  @ room temperature
2 tbs granulated sugar
½ tsp vanilla extract
2 tbs all purpose flour
1 large egg
1 large egg yolk
½ cup pineapple curd (recipe
  on page 118)
½ cup flaked coconut

Prep:
Set up AquaChef by filling the water basin with water to the minimum fill line and turn on the AquaChef to preheat to 165°F.

Using stand mixer or hand mixer place cream cheese into bowl and mix for 1-2 minutes alone.

Add the granulated sugar, vanilla extract, and flour. Mix well being sure all ingredients are incorporated.

Scrape down the bowl and add the egg. Make sure it is completely incorporated before adding the yolk.

Add the yolk and set aside.

Gently fold in the pineapple curd and flaked coconut.

Continue on next page...

Pineapple Coconut Cheesecake (continued)

Prep:
Divide between the ramekins/mason jars. If using mason jars cover with mason jar lids. Place each in the preheated AquaChef.

Cook the Pineapple Coconut Cheesecake for 2 hours at 165°F.

Finishing:
Carefully remove the Pineapple Coconut Cheese Cake and refrigerate for 6-8 hours before serving. Serve with fresh whipped cream and pineapple curd. Enjoy!

Tips:
Toasting the flaked coconut before adding to the cheesecake batter adds great texture to the cheesecake!

Strawberries With Angel Food Cake

Time: 1 hour
Temperature: 185°F
Serves: 2

Items Needed:
ramekins
mixing bowl
whisk

7-8 thinly sliced strawberries
1 box of angel food cake mix
1 20 oz can crushed pineapple
   with the juice

Prep:
Set up AquaChef by filling the water basin with 9 cups of water
and turn on the AquaChef to preheat to 185°F.

Line each ramekin with an even layer of the sliced strawberries.

In the mixing bowl place the angel food cake mix and the can of
crushed pineapple with the juice; using the whisk combine the cake
mix with the crushed pineapple.

Once the cake mix is mixed well with the crushed pineapple pour
into each ramekin being sure not to fill above ¾ of the way (we
need to give the cake room to rise).

Continue on next page...

Strawberries With Angel Food Cake
(continued)

Prep:
Place each ramekin in the preheated AquaChef.

Cook the Strawberries with Angel Food Cake for 1 hour at 185°F.

Finishing:
Carefully remove each ramekin and serve with whipped cream or eat alone. Enjoy!

Tips:
The cake mix makes a large volume. You can choose to cook this dessert in 16 oz mason jars or you can save the batter and cook more as the ramekins become available.

White Chocolate Raspberry Cheese Cake

Time: 1 hour
Non Cooking Time: 6-8 hours
Temperature: 165°F
Serves: 3-4

Items Needed:
stand or hand mixer
rubber spatula
3-4 ramekins

8 oz cream cheese @ room temperature
2 tbs sugar
1 tsp vanilla extract
2 tbs all purpose flour
1 large egg
1 large egg yolk
½ cup white chocolate chips
¾ cup fresh raspberries

Prep:
Set up AquaChef by filling the water basin with 9 cups of water and turn on the AquaChef to preheat to 165°F.

Using stand mixer or hand mixer mix cream cheese for 1-2 minutes alone. Add the granulated sugar, vanilla extract, and flour. Mix well being sure all ingredients are incorporated. Scrape down the bowl and add the egg.

Make sure it is completely incorporated before adding the yolk. Add the yolk and mix well until all is incorporated.

Gently fold in the white chocolate chips and the raspberries.

Divide the batter and place into each ramekin; using the rubber spatula smooth the tops of each ramekin.

Continue on next page...

White Chocolate Raspberry Cheese Cake (continued)

Prep:
Place each in the preheated AquaChef.

Cook the White Chocolate Raspberry Cheesecake for 1 hour at 165°F.

Finishing:
Carefully remove the White Chocolate Raspberry Cheesecakes and refrigerate for 6-8 hours before serving. Once chilled, Enjoy!

Tips:
If you are not able to use fresh raspberries you may use frozen raspberries. If using frozen toss the frozen raspberries in 1 tbs all purpose flour before folding into the cheesecake batter.

Oatmeal

Oatmeal is a grain product which has a nutty flavor when cooked. Known for its health benefits because of its high content of complex carbohydrates and water soluble fibre, oatmeal can make a tasty and healthy breakfast or dessert.

Berry Oatmeal

Time: 1 hour
Temperature: 175°F
Serves: 2

Items Needed:
mixing bowl
small bowl
spoon for mixing
mason jars with lids

1 cup rolled oats
2 tbs brown sugar
½ teaspoon cinnamon
2 eggs
3/4 cup almond milk or coconut
  milk
1 cup frozen mixed berries
1 tsp all purpose flour

Prep:
Set up AquaChef by filling the water basin with water to the minimum fill line and turn on the AquaChef to preheat to 175°F. In large mixing bowl place oats, brown sugar, and cinnamon. Mix the ingredients together. Add the eggs, and almond milk. In a separate bowl place frozen berries with 1 tsp of flour. Toss around being sure all berries are coated with the flour. Gently stir in the flour coated berries. Divide and place the batter in each mason jar. Cover the mason jars and place in the preheated AquaChef. Cook the Berry Oatmeal at 175°F for 1 Hour.

Finishing:
Carefully remove the Berry Oatmeal and enjoy!

Tips:
This dairy-free breakfast item can be enjoyed any time of the day, as an afternoon snack or a light dinner option!

Jared's Pumpkin Oatmeal

Time: 1 hour
Temperature: 175°F
Serves: 4

Items Needed:
mixing bowl
spoon for mixing
mason jars with lids

2 cups old fashioned
   rolled oats
2 tbs brown sugar
¼ tsp ground cinnamon
½ tsp pumpkin pie spice
pinch of salt
1 egg
¾ cup pumpkin puree
¾ cup almond milk

Prep:
Set up AquaChef by filling the water basin with water to the minimum fill line and turn on the AquaChef to preheat to 175°F. Place oats, brown sugar, pumpkin pie spice, cinnamon, and salt into mixing bowl. Mix all the ingredients together making sure all the spices are distributed. Add the egg, pumpkin puree, and almond milk and mix well. Divide the mixture among the mason jars, cover each mason jar and place in the preheated AquaChef. Cook Jared's Pumpkin Oatmeal for 1 hour at 175°F.

Finishing:
Carefully remove and enjoy!

Tips:
Try adding 2 tbs chia seeds to the mixture before cooking. This dairy-free treat will keep you full until lunch!

Zucchini Chocolate Oatmeal

Time: 1 hour
Temperature: 175°F
Serves: 2

Items Needed:
grater
mixing bowl
spoon for mixing
2 pint mason jars with lids

1 medium size zucchini
¼ cup semi sweet chocolate chips
1 large egg
1 tbs brown sugar
¾ cup coconut milk
1 cup old fashioned rolled oats

Prep:
Set up AquaChef by filling the water basin with water to the minimum fill line and turn on the AquaChef to preheat to 175°F. Remove the top and bottom of the zucchini, and grate the zucchini into the mixing bowl. Add the chocolate chips, egg, brown sugar, and coconut milk. Mix the ingredients well before adding the oats. Add the oats and make sure all the ingredients are well incorporated, divide and place ½ the mixture in each mason jar. Cover each mason jar and place in the preheated AquaChef. Cook the Zucchini Chocolate Oatmeal for 1 hour at 175°F.

Finishing:
Carefully remove the Zucchini Chocolate Oatmeal and enjoy!

Tips:
Adding zucchini to this tasty oatmeal is a great way to sneak vegetables into picky eaters. I suggest grating it fine.

Pudding

Dessert puddings are a comfort food favorite! Most often including milk and sugar with a thickening agent in order to create a sweet, creamy dessert, puddings are easy to make and tasty to eat!

Brownie Bread Pudding

Time: 2 hours
Temperature: 175°F
Serves: 4

Items Needed:
two mixing bowls
whisk; rubber spatula
4 ramekins/mason jars
mason jar lids

wet ingredients:
½ cup heavy cream
2 egg yolks
1 whole egg
1 tbs granulated sugar
¼ cup cooled
chocolate sauce (see
  page 98)
½ tsp vanilla extract

dry ingredients:
16 oz brownies at room
temperature

Prep:
Set up AquaChef by filling the water basin with 9 cups of water and turn on the AquaChef to preheat to 175°F.

In one mixing bowl place all the wet ingredients and gently whisk together; set aside. Cut brownies into 1 inch cubes and place into second mixing bowl. Once all brownies are cubed add the wet ingredients and gently stir together.

Divide the mixture between the ramekins/mason jars. If using mason jars use the mason jar lids. Once all are covered place in the preheated AquaChef. Cook the Brownie Bread Pudding for 2 hours at 175°F.

Continue on next page...

Brownie Bread Pudding (continued)

Finishing:
Carefully remove the Brownie Bread Pudding and serve warm with either the AquaChef Vanilla Anglaise or vanilla ice cream. Enjoy!

Tips:
If you do not have time to make your own brownies, using store bought will save you time.

Buttermilk Custard Pudding

Time: 1 hour
Non Cook Time: 6-8 hours
Temperature: 180°F
Serves: 2

Items Needed:
mixing bowl
whisk
strainer or food sieve
3-4 half pint mason jars or
  8 oz ramekins
mason jar lids

4 large egg yolks
1 cup buttermilk
½ cup granulated sugar
½ cup packed brown sugar
½ cup maple syrup

Prep:
Set up AquaChef by filling the water basin with 9 cups of water and turn on the AquaChef to preheat to 180°F.

Place the yolks into the mixing bowl. Break up the egg yolks with the whisk and add the buttermilk; gently whisk together. Add the granulated sugar, brown sugar, and maple syrup. Once all combined strain using the metal sieve and pour into mason jars or ramekins. Cover each and place in the preheated AquaChef. Cook the Buttermilk Custard Pudding for 1 hour at 180°F.

Continue on next page...

Buttermilk Custard Pudding (continued)

Finishing:
Carefully remove the Buttermilk Custard Pudding and refrigerate for 6-8 hours before serving. Enjoy!

Tips:
Serve with candied pecans and whipped cream.

Caramel Apple Bread Pudding

Time: 3 hours
Temperature: 175°F
Serves: 4

Items Needed:
vegetable peeler
mixing bowl
spoon/rubber spatula
4 ramekins

1 large Granny Smith apple
¼ cup Dulce de leche sauce
¼ tsp ground cinnamon

wet ingredients:
½ cup heavy cream
2 egg yolks
2 tbs granulated sugar
½ tsp bourbon vanilla
dry ingredients:
4-6 slices of cinnamon
bread (cubed)

Prep:
Set up AquaChef by filling the water basin with 9 cups of water and turn on the AquaChef to preheat to 175°F. Begin by peeling the Granny Smith apple and cube the apple into ½ inch cubes. Place the cut apples in the small mixing bowl, add the Dulce de leche sauce and cinnamon. Place the combined ingredients into a Seal N Fresh bag, seal the bag using the Seal N Fresh vacuum sealer and place in the preheated AquaChef and cook for 1 hour. Once the apples are done cooking carefully remove and set aside. Combine all the wet ingredients. Add the apples and cubed cinnamon bread to wet ingredients and gently mix together; divide the mixture and place in the ramekins. Place each ramekin into the preheated AquaChef. Cook the Caramel Apple Bread Pudding for 2 hours at 175°F.

Finishing:
Carefully remove Caramel Apple Bread Pudding and enjoy!

Eggnog Bread Pudding

Time: 2 hours
Temperature: 175°F
Serves: 4
Items Needed:
mixing bowl
whisk
spoon/rubber spatula
4 ramekins

dry ingredients:
6 slices of cinnamon bread
wet ingredients:
½ cup heavy cream
2 egg yolks
2 tbs granulated sugar
¼ tsp ground cloves
¼ tsp ground nutmeg
¼ tsp ground cinnamon
½ tsp bourbon vanilla

Prep:
Set up AquaChef by filling the water basin with 9 cups of water and turn on the AquaChef to preheat to 175°F.

Begin by cutting the cinnamon bread into ½-1 inch cubes; set aside the cubed bread. In mixing bowl combine the wet ingredients and whisk together. Gently fold in the cubed cinnamon bread. Once combined divide the mixture into the ramekins. Place each ramekin into the preheated AquaChef.

Cook the Eggnog Bread Pudding for 2 hours at 175°F.

Finishing:
Carefully remove the Eggnog Bread Pudding and serve with the Eggnog Creme Anglaise. Enjoy!

Vanilla Raisin Bread Pudding

Time: 1 hour
Temperature: 170°F
Serves: 2

Items Needed:
mixing bowl
whisk
spoon/rubber spatula
2 ramekins

wet ingredients:
½ cup heavy cream
2 egg yolks
2 tbs granulated sugar
½ tsp bourbon vanilla
dry ingredients:
4-5 slices cinnamon raisin
texas toast (sliced double
the size of normal bread)

Prep:
Set up AquaChef by filling the water basin with 9 cups of water
and turn on the AquaChef to preheat to 170°F. In a mixing bowl
combine all the wet ingredients and set aside. Take the bread and
cut into 1 inch cubes. Add the cubed bread to the wet ingredients
and lightly mix. Divide the mixture between the two ramekins.
Place the Vanilla Raisin Bread Pudding in the preheated AquaChef.
Cook the Vanilla Raisin Bread Pudding for 1 hour at 170°F.

Finishing:
Carefully remove the Vanilla Raisin Bread Pudding and enjoy!

Tips:
Serve with fresh whipped cream or the AquaChef Vanilla Anglaise.

Sweet or Savory Sweet Potatoes

Time: 1 hour 30 min
Temperature: 170°F
Serves: 4-5

Items Needed:
optional vegetable peeler
optional vegetable scrubber

2 medium to large
  sweet potatoes
sweet:
  ⅓ cup raisins
  ½ cup packed brown sugar
  1 tsp ground cinnamon
  ¼ cup unsalted butter (cubed)
or **savory:**
  ½ tsp minced ginger
  2 tsp minced garlic
  ½ tsp turmeric
  ¼ cup unsalted butter (cubed)
  salt and pepper to taste

Prep:
Set up AquaChef by filling the water basin with water to the max
fill line and turn on the AquaChef to preheat to 170°F. Clean the
sweet potatoes being sure to remove any debris and dirt. Next peel
and cube the sweet potatoes. Place in a large Seal N Fresh bag.
Add the remaining ingredients if you are making sweet or savory.
Seal using the Seal N Fresh vacuum sealer and place in the preheated AquaChef. Cook the Sweet or Savory Sweet Potatoes for 1
hour and 30 minutes at 170°F.

Finishing:
Remove from the bag and serve with your favorite main dish.
Enjoy!

Tips:
Questions about this recipe? View the quick tip video on gourmet
cooking online.

Poaching

While poaching itself is merely a process of gently simmering food in liquid, with desserts poaching can be a perfect option to create delicious treats for those cold winter nights. Often simmered in alcohol, and cooked at the perfect temperature the *sous vide* way, the poached dessert is tender and flavorful and will warm you from the inside out!

Champagne Poached Pears

Time: 2 hours 30 minutes
Non Cooking Time: 1 hour
Temperature: 180°F
Serves: 4

Items Needed:
stand or hand mixer
sauce pan

4 red pears
1 tsp vanilla extract
1 cinnamon stick
½ cup sugar
1 bottle dry champagne
1 cup heavy whipping cream

Prep:
Set up AquaChef by filling the water basin with water to the max fill line and turn on the AquaChef to preheat to 180°F.

Begin by peeling the pears and carefully remove the core through the bottom keeping the top of the pear intact. Once done with all pears place the peeled and cored pears in a large Seal N Fresh bag.

To the bag add vanilla extract, cinnamon stick, sugar, and champagne. Close the top of the bag leaving a 1-2 inch opening for the bubbles to release during cooking. Place the bag in the preheated AquaChef.

Cook the Champagne Poached Pears for 2 hours and 30 minutes at 180°F.

Continue on next page...

Champagne Poached Pears (continued)

Finishing:
Carefully remove the bag and place the poaching liquid into a sauce pan. Place the saucepan on low-medium heat and reduce the liquid by ¾.

Once the liquid is reduced cool the liquid by placing into the refrigerator. Once the liquid is cool make whipped cream with the heavy cream, using a stand or hand mixer.

Once the cream is at soft peaks add ¼ cup of the reduced liquid; continue mixing, add an additional ¼ cup.

Serve the Champagne Poached Pears with this cream and drizzle more of the reduced poaching liquid on top of the pears. Enjoy!

Shiraz Poached Pears

Time: 2 hours 30 minutes
Temperature: 180°F
Serves: 4

Items Needed:
vegetable peeler
melon baller
saucepan

4 bartlett pears
1 bottle Shiraz red wine
 (use any red you prefer)
½ cup maple syrup
¼ cup granulated sugar
3-4 star anise

Prep:
Set up AquaChef by filling the water basin with water to the max fill line and turn on the AquaChef to preheat to 180°F. Begin by peeling each pear. Once all the pears are peeled remove the core from the bottom Keeping the stem attached for presentation. Place each peeled and cored pear into a large Seal N Fresh bag, add the remaining ingredients to the bag and seal the top. Gently agitate the bag to make sure all the ingredients are incorporated. Place into the preheated AquaChef. Cook the Shiraz Poached Pears for 2 hours and 30 minutes at 180°F.

Finishing:
Carefully remove the pears and place the poaching liquid into the saucepan and reduce the liquid by ½. Serve the pears with the sauce made from the poaching liquid. Enjoy!

Tips:
If you are not a fan of star anise you can substitute a cinnamon stick and cloves.

Shiraz Poached Pears

Spiced Rum Poached Pears

Time: 2 hours 30 min
Temperature: 180°F
Serves: 2

Items Needed:
vegetable peeler
melon baller

2 bosc pears
¼ cup spiced dark rum
(we used Sailor Jerry's rum)
1 cup fresh squeezed
  orange juice
½-1 cup of water
1 cup packed brown sugar
peel of 1 orange
1 tsp vanilla extract
1 cinnamon stick

Prep:
Set up AquaChef by filling the water basin with water to the max fill line and turn on the AquaChef to preheat to 180°F. Begin by peeling the pears and coring from the bottom. I keep the stem of the pear on for decorative purposes. Place the peeled and cored pears in a large Seal N Fresh Bag. Add the liquid ingredients to the bag. Once all the liquid ingredients are in the bag add the remaining ingredients and seal the top of the bag. Gently agitate the bag once the top is sealed to make sure all the ingredients are incorporated. Place the pears in the preheated AquaChef. Cook the Spiced Rum Poached Pears for 2 hours and 30 minutes at 180°F.

Finishing:
Carefully remove the Spiced Rum Poached Pears and serve with vanilla ice cream or fresh whipped cream. Enjoy!

Tips:
Turn the poaching liquid into a sauce for this dessert by placing the liquid into a saucepan and reducing the sauce by ¾ until thickened.

Sauces

Dessert sauces are usually sweet and invariably delicious. Usually not served by themselves, they add flavor, moisture, and visual appeal to other dishes. Here we review the preparation of delicious dessert sauces that can be mixed and matched with other desserts.

Chocolate Sauce

Time: 15 minutes
Non Cooking Time: 2-4 hours
Temperature: 165°F
Serves: 3-4

1 cup semisweet chocolate chips
¾ cup heavy whipping cream
pinch of salt

Items Needed:
rubber spatula

Prep:
Set up AquaChef by filling the water basin with water to the max fill line and turn on the AquaChef to preheat to 165°F. In a small Seal N Fresh bag place chocolate chips, heavy cream, and salt. Seal the top of the bag and place in the preheated AquaChef.

Finishing:
Remove the bag and carefully open; using the rubber spatula mix together until smooth. Serve the chocolate sauce with any of your favorite desserts.

Tips:
Store in an airtight container for up to one week.
This sauce will be used for the Brownie Bread Pudding

Strawberry Sauce

Time: 30 minutes
Temperature: 175°F
Serves: 2-4

Items Needed:
blender or burr mixer

1 cup fresh or frozen
    strawberries
2 tbs granulated sugar
¼ tsp vanilla extract

Prep:
Set up AquaChef by filling the water basin with water to the max fill line and turn on the AquaChef to preheat to 175°F. If using fresh strawberries be sure to rinse and remove the tops of the strawberries. Place the strawberries in a small Seal N Fresh bag, add the sugar and vanilla extract. Seal the bag using the Seal N Fresh Vacuum Sealer and place in the preheated AquaChef. Cook the strawberries for 30 minutes at 175°F.

Finishing:
Carefully remove the strawberries and juices and place in blender and blend until smooth. Chill the sauce for 1 hour before using. Serve with the AquaChef Panna cotta. Enjoy!

Tips:
You can strain the sauce with a metal sieve to remove the seeds and make a smoother sauce.

Pot de Crème

&

Clotted Cream

Pot de Crème is a loose French dessert custard that has been made for centuries. Custard preparation is a delicate operation, because a temperature increase of 5–10 °F (3-6 °C) leads to overcooking and curdling. Thus, because of its precision temperature control, the *sous vide* method is the ideal way to cook custards!

Here we also see how to make clotted cream. A great dessert substitute for crème fraîche, clotted cream is similar to sour cream, but less sour and more rich.

Butterscotch Pot De Crème

Time: 1 hour
Non Cooking time: 3-7 hours
Temperature: 115°F and
160°F
Serves: 2-3

½ cup heavy cream
½ cup crème fraiche
3 oz butterscotch chips
1 tbs vanilla sugar
pinch of salt
4 large egg yolks

Prep:
Set up AquaChef by filling the water basin with water to the max fill line and turn on the AquaChef to preheat to 115°F. Place heavy cream, crème fraiche, and butterscotch chips in a Seal N Fresh bag. Place in AquaChef at 115°F for 20 min or until chips are melted. Once melted incorporate ingredients by mixing around in bag. In a mixing bowl lightly beat egg yolks, sugar, and salt together. Add yolk mixture to bag and place in the AquaChef. Increase heat to 160°F and cook for 50 min.

Finishing:
After cooking pour or scoop the butterscotch crème into a refrigerator safe bowl or container (ex: champagne flute) and chill for 3-7 hours.

Tips:
Serve with whipped cream. Optional: top with crushed gingersnap cookies.

Chocolate Pot De Crème

Time: 1 hour 30 minutes
Temperature: 115°F then
165°F
Serves: 4

Items Needed:
small whisk

1 cup heavy whipping cream
½ cup semisweet chocolate
chips
2 tbs sugar
3 large egg yolks
1 whole large egg
pinch of salt

Prep:
Set up AquaChef by filling the water basin with water to the max fill line and turn on the AquaChef to preheat to 115°F. Place the heavy whipping cream and chocolate chips in a Seal N Fresh bag and seal the top. Place inside the preheated AquaChef and heat through for 20-30 minutes or until the chocolate chips are melted. Once melted add the remaining ingredients to the bag and whisk gently together. Turn the heat up on the AquaChef to 165°F, seal the top of the bag and place in the AquaChef.
Cook the Chocolate Pot de Crème for 1 hour at 165°F.

Finishing:
Remove the bag and pour or scoop the chocolate crème into a refrigerator safe bowl or container (ex: champagne flute) and chill for 3-7 hours.

Tips:
Save the egg whites and cook a sundried tomato egg white frittata.

Clotted Cream

Time: 10 hours   16 oz heavy whipping cream
Temperature: 180°F
Serves: 5-6

Items Needed:
2 8 oz mason jars with lids

Prep:
Set up AquaChef by filling the water basin with water to the max fill line and turn on the AquaChef to preheat to 180°F. Fill each mason jar with 8 oz/1 Cup of heavy whipping cream, cover with lid and place in preheated AquaChef. Add more water if needed, best to have water all the way to the line of the heavy cream. Cook the clotted cream for 10 hours at 180°F.

Finishing:
When the cream is finished cooking, being extra careful not to disturb the cream, place in the refrigerator overnight for the cream to set. Using a slotted spoon remove the clotted cream from the whey and store in a separate clean container. Serve the clotted cream alone or with your favorite pastries. Enjoy!

Tips:
If you have a recipe that calls for crème fraiche you can use clotted cream as a replacement.

Everyday Desserts made Gourmet:
The Sous Vide way

Crisps

&

Crumbles

Fruit crisps are a type of dessert usually consisting of fruit baked with a crispy topping. These desserts have become an American and British tradition and are also very popular in Canada, especially in areas where berries and fruit are readily available. Try these recipes and you'll see why for yourself!

Cranberry Crisp

Time: 1 hour 30 minutes
Temperature: 175°F
Serves: 2

Items Needed:
food processor
oven preheated to 350°F
sheet pan; parchment paper
2 ramekins/mason jars
mason jar lids

8 oz fresh cranberries
¼ cup granulated sugar
pinch of salt
crisp topping:
    ¼ cup unsalted butter
    (Chilled and Cubed)
    ¼ cup all purpose flour
    ¼ cup rolled oats
    ½ cup chopped pecans
    ½ tsp ground cinnamon
    1 tbs honey

Prep:
Set up AquaChef by filling the water basin with 9 cups of water and turn on the AquaChef to preheat to 175°F. Rinse and dry the cranberries, place in the food processor. Add the sugar and salt. Lightly chop the cranberries (medium pieces); divide the chopped cranberries and place into the ramekins/ mason jars. Cover each and place into the preheated AquaChef. Cook the cranberries for 1 hour and 30 minutes at 175°F.

Continue on next page...

Cranberry Crisp (continued)

Finishing:
While the cranberries are cooking begin to make the crisp topping. Into the food processor place cubed and chilled butter, all purpose flour, rolled oats, chopped pecans, cinnamon, and honey. Pulse together until combined. Place mixture onto a parchment lined sheet pan and place in the preheated oven. Cook until golden brown; this should take 15-20 Minutes. Once the cranberries have finished cooking in the AquaChef carefully remove and top with the crisp. Enjoy!

Tips:
If you are not able to find fresh cranberries frozen can be used.

Cranberry Crisp

Pear Crisp

Time: 2 hours
Temperature: 185°F
Serves: 2

Items Needed:
vegetable peeler
melon baller or apple corer
mixing bowl
food processor
oven preheated to 350°F
sheet pan
parchment paper
2 ramekins/mason jars
mason jar lids

2 D'anjou pears
½ cup brown sugar
2 tbs unsalted butter (melted)
¼ tsp ground clove
½ tsp ground cinnamon
crisp topping:
    ¼ cup unsalted butter
     (chilled and cubed)
    ¼ cup all purpose flour
    ¼ cup rolled oats
    ½ cup chopped pecans
    ½ tsp ground cinnamon
    1 tbs honey

Prep:
Set up AquaChef by filling the water basin with 9 cups of water and turn on the AquaChef to preheat to 185°F.

Begin by removing the core of each pear, then remove the peel.

Cut the pears in ½ length wise, then slice thinly.

Place the sliced pears in the mixing bowl; add brown sugar, melted butter, clove, and cinnamon.

Gently coat the pear slices and layer into the ramekins/mason jars.

Continue on next page...

Pear Crisp (continued)

Once each is filled cover with mason lid. Place each in the preheated AquaChef.

Finishing:
While the pears are cooking in the AquaChef begin to make the crisp topping. Place cubed and chilled butter, all purpose flour, rolled oats, chopped pecans, cinnamon, and honey into the food processor. Pulse together until combined. Place mixture onto a parchment lined sheet pan and place in the preheated oven. Cook until golden brown. This should take 15-20 minutes. When the pears are done cooking top with the crisp. Enjoy!

Curds

Curds are dessert spreads and toppings made with various fruits. The basic ingredients are egg yolks, sugar, fruit juice and zest. A dairy product, curds are obtained by curdling milk with an acidic substance such as lemon juice or vinegar, and then draining off the liquid portion. The increased acidity causes the milk proteins to tangle into solid masses which are called *curds*. For hundreds of years this simple method has been used to make unique and delicious desserts. Now we can take these recipes to a whole new level with the perfect temperature control offered by cooking the *sous vide* way.

Lemon Curd

Time: 1 hour
Temperature: 180°F
Serves: 5-6

Items Needed:
mixing bowls
hand mixer/stand mixer
sauce pan
2 ½ pint mason jars with lids

4 large egg yolks
½ cup sugar
pinch of salt
½ cup fresh squeezed
   lemon juice
4 oz unsalted butter, melted
   (½ stick)

Prep:
Set up AquaChef by filling the water basin with water to the minimum fill line and turn on the AquaChef to preheat to 180°F. In mixing bowl or stand mixer combine eggs, sugar, and salt. Mix thoroughly until sugar is dissolved and the batter is slightly thickened being sure not to create a foam. Combine lemon juice and melted butter to the egg mixture. Pour the mixture into each mason jar and cover with lid. Place each filled jar in the preheated AquaChef. Cook the lemon curd for 1 hour at 180°F.

Finishing:
Remove and place the lemon curd into an ice bath for 15-20 min. Place in the refrigerator after opening. Serve with pound cake or any dessert you choose. Enjoy!

Tips:
If you enjoy other citrus such as lime or oranges you can substitute and make lime or orange curd.

Lemon Curd Pudding Cake

Time: 1 hour
Temperature: 200°F
Serves: 2

Items Needed:
2 mixing bowls
whisk; 2 ramekins

dry ingredients:
½ cup all purpose flour
2 tbs granulated sugar
pinch of salt

wet ingredients:
1 large egg
3 tbs vegetable oil
3 tbs lemon curd
1 tbs heavy cream
zest of 1 lemon

Prep:
Set up AquaChef by filling the water basin with 9 cups of water and turn on the AquaChef to preheat to 200°F. In one mixing bowl place all dry ingredients and set aside. In separate mixing bowl add egg, vegetable oil, lemon curd, heavy cream, and zest. Mix well with whisk being sure all are incorporated. Slowly add dry ingredients being sure to whisk out any lumps. Once all ingredients are incorporated divide between the two ramekins. Place each in the preheated AquaChef. Cook the Lemon Curd Pudding Cake for 1 hour at 200°F.

Finishing:
Remove each from the AquaChef. Serve with whipped cream and more lemon curd if you like. Enjoy!

Pineapple Curd

Time: 1 hour
Cook time on stove top:
  20-30 minutes
Temperature: 180°F
Serves: 5-6

Items Needed:
2 mixing bowls
hand mixer/stand mixer
burr mixer or blender
sauce pan
slotted spoon
food sieve
2-3 pint size mason jars

1 1/2 lb fresh pineapple
  (cut into 1-2 in cubes)
3 tbs water
1 cup unsalted butter (melted)
½ cup sugar
3 large eggs
pinch of salt

Prep:
Set up AquaChef by filling the water basin with water to the minimum fill line and turn on the AquaChef to preheat to 180°F.

Place the cubed pineapple in the saucepan and add 3 tbs of water. Begin to cook on medium heat. Once the pineapple has started to break down turn off heat.

Using either the burr or blender carefully puree the cooked pineapple. Once pureed strain though the food sieve. You will want 1 ¼- 1 ½ cup of strained pineapple. Setting the strained pineapple aside, whisk the eggs, sugar, and salt together until all is dissolved and thickened slightly. Add the strained pineapple and melted butter; mix well together.

Continue on next page...

Pineapple Curd (continued)

Items Needed:
Pour into mason jars and cover with lids. Place into the preheated AquaChef. Cook the pineapple curd for 1 hour at 180°F.

Finishing:
Turn off the AquaChef and place ice cubes into the water basin creating an ice bath for the pineapple curd. Once cooled place in the refrigerator. Serve as a topping on cake or ice cream. Enjoy!

Tips:
The pineapple curd will be used for the Pineapple Apricot Cake.

Strawberries Curd

Time: 1 hour
Temperature: 180°F
Serves: 5-6

Items Needed:
2 mixing bowls
hand mixer/stand mixer
sauce pan
slotted spoon
food sieve
2-3 pint size mason jars

1 1/2 lb strawberries
(cleaned and halved, weight should be taken after cleaning)
3 tbs water
1 cup unsalted butter (melted)
½ cup sugar
3 large eggs
pinch of salt

Prep:
Set up AquaChef by filling the water basin with water to the minimum fill line and turn on the AquaChef to preheat to 180°F.

Place the cleaned strawberries in the saucepan and add 3 tbs of water. Cook on medium heat. Once the strawberries have started to break down turn off heat. Using the food sieve and slotted spoon scoop the strawberries and run through the sieve. Use the spoon to help get the strawberries through the sieve. Once all the strawberries are through the sieve set aside. Whisk the eggs, sugar, and salt until dissolved and thickened slightly. Add the strained strawberries and melted butter, mix well. Place in the mason jars and cover. Place the filled mason jars in the preheated AquaChef.

Cook the strawberry curd for 1 hour at 180°F.

Continue on next page...

Strawberries Curd (continued)

Finishing:

Turn off the AquaChef and place ice cubes into the water basin creating an ice bath for the strawberry curd. Some water may need to be removed to make room for the ice cubes. Once cooled place in the refrigerator. Serve on top of ice cream or vanilla custard. This goes great with the clotted cream. Enjoy!

Tips:

Strawberry curd makes a wonderful food gift and lasts up to two months in the refrigerator.

About Chef Mel

After a youthful love affair with all things Julia Child, Melissa Silva-Torcedo catapulted her passion and love for the art of cooking into a successful career in the food industry starting in 2003. At the inspiration of her muse she graduated from Le Cordon Bleu in Pasadena, California in 2005.

Before hosting Cooking with Mel, Melissa put her cooking skills to work at 5-Star Restaurants in Los Angeles and San Diego, working alongside some of the best Chefs in the industry. She's also an author of two gourmet cookbooks.

Everyday Desserts
made Gourmet:
The Sous Vide way

Says Chef Mel, "Showing people how to turn ordinary food into extraordinary meals – that's my passion. Home cooked gourmet meals can not only be quick & easy-to-make, but affordable too."

Always the willing hostess and at her family's behest, Melissa caters to family and friends on a regular basis, to cries of "More! More!" for her signature dish of Macaroni and Cheese. Chef Mel's baking skills are also eagerly sought for birthday confections – especially her delicious cupcakes.

Melissa enjoys frequenting local restaurants to sample what's new and fresh in the industry, often recreating her favorites with her own unique twist!

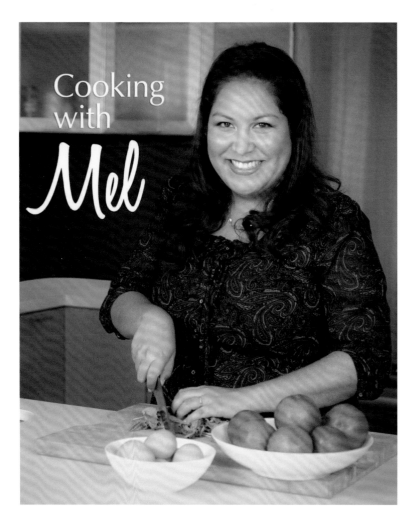

Everyday Desserts made *Gourmet:* The Sous Vide way

Index

A

almond
  milk
    Berry Oatmeal   74
    Jared's Pumpkin Oatmeal   75
angel food cake mix
    Strawberries with Angel Food Cake   67
Apples
  Granny Smith
    AquaChef Dulce de leche Apples   18
    Caramel Apple Bread Pudding   84

B

bell peppers
    Fire Roasted Bell Pepper Ricotta Cheesecake   59
berries
  mixed
    Berry Oatmeal   74
bourbon vanilla
    Caramel Apple Bread Pudding   84
    Eggnog Bread Pudding   85
    Vanilla Raisin Bread Pudding   86
bread
  cinnamon
    Caramel Apple Bread Pudding   84
    Eggnog Bread Pudding   85
  cinnamon raisin
    Vanilla Raisin Bread Pudding   86
brownies
    Brownie Bread Pudding   80
butter
  unsalted
    Corn Bread Pudding Cake   54
    Cranberry Crisp   108
    Gingerbread Pudding Cake   61
    Pear Crisp   111
    Pineapple and Apricot Pudding Cake   63
    Pineapple Curd   118
    Strawberries Curd   120
    Sweet or Savory Sweet Potatoes   87
buttermilk
    Buttermilk Custard Pudding   82
butterscotch chips
    Butterscotch Pot de Creme   102
butterscotch morsels
    Butterscotch Custard   38

C

champagne
    Champagne Poached Pears   90

cheese
  cheddar
    Corn Bread Pudding Cake   54
  ricotta
    Fire Roasted Bell Pepper Ricotta Cheesecake   59
chinese 5 spice
    Gingerbread Pudding Cake   61
chives
    Corn Bread Pudding Cake   54
chocolate chips
  semi sweet
    Chocolate Custard   41
    Chocolate Pot de Creme   103
    Chocolate Sauce   98
    Zucchini Chocolate Oatmeal   76
  white
    White Chocolate Raspberry Cheese Cake   69
chocolate sauce
    Brownie Bread Pudding   80
cinnamon
    Berry Oatmeal   74
    Caramel Apple Bread Pudding   84
    Cranberry Crisp   108
    Date and Walnut Cheesecake   56
    Dulce de leche Apples   18
    Dulce de leche Rice Pudding   19
    Eggnog Bread Pudding   85
    Eggnog Creme Anglaise   43
    Gingerbread Pudding cake   61
    Jared's Pumpkin Oatmeal   75
    Pear Crisp   111
    Pumpkin Custard   44
    Sweet or Savory Sweet Potatoes   87
cinnamon stick
    Champagne Poached Pears   90
    Spiced Rum Poached Pears   94
cloves
  ground
    Eggnog Bread Pudding   85
    Pear Crisp   111
  whole
    Eggnog Creme Anglaise   43
coconut
  flaked
    Pineapple Coconut Cheesecake   65
  milk
    Berry Oatmeal   74
    Pumpkin Custard   44
    Zucchini Chocolate Oatmeal   76
coffee
  grounds
    Coffee Panna cotta   27
corn
  creamed
    Corn Bread Pudding Cake   54